Becoming the Parent Your Child Needs

Becoming the Parent Your Child Needs

Joyce Marie Smith

TYNDALE HOUSE PUBLISHERS, INC.
Wheaton, Illinois

Third printing, November 1982

Library of Congress Catalog Card Number 79-92971
ISBN 0-8423-0133-X, paper
Copyright © 1980 by Joyce Marie Smith
All rights reserved
Printed in the United States of America.

*TO OUR CHILDREN,
GAYLENE, SHELLY, LORI, AND GREG—
Precious Gifts From God.*

Contents

Acknowledgments 9

Preface 11

Called to Parenthood
 1. You the Parent 13
 2. Parental Responsibilities 17
 3. Disciping Your Child 21

Called to Develop and Train
 4. Developing Your Child's Self-Esteem 26
 5. Developing Character and Values 30
 6. Developing Your Child's Uniqueness and Gifts 34

Called to Discipline
 7. Disciplining Toward Obedience 37
 8. Disciplining Older Children 41
 9. Special Discipline Problems 45

Called to Completion
10. Family Oneness 50
11. Preparation for Independence 54
12. Parental Prayers 58

Acknowledgments

Proverbs 24:3, 4 From the *Amplified Bible,* Old Testament, Part II, Copyright 1962 by Zondervan Publishing House.

Genesis 7:1; 17:7; 28:14; Joshua 24:15; Ephesians 4:3. Scripture quotations are from the *New American Standard Bible,* ® The Lockman Foundation 1960, 1962, 1963, 1968, 1971, 1972, 1973, 1975.

Proverbs 20:11 and Ezekiel 11:19 taken from *The Living Bible,* copyright 1971 by Tyndale House Publishers, Wheaton, Ill. Used by permission.

Preface

Parenting can be an exciting and rewarding experience or it can be a painful trauma. So much depends upon our attitudes as parents, our own relationship to God, and the application of biblical principles in our homes.

This study will help you develop confidence as a parent and give you biblical direction as you grow in your God-given responsibilities.

Becoming the Parent Your Child Needs can be used as an individual study, as a small group Bible study, or in a Sunday school class.

Called to Parenthood
Lesson One
You the Parent

Parenting involves a combination of hard work and fun; pride and humility; consistency and flexibility; teaching and learning; tears of sorrow and tears of joy; and a great deal of prayer. Parenting is an exciting adventure, but also a tremendous responsibility.

Planning Ahead

1. What do you think are necessary qualities in establishing a godly home? _____
   _____
   _____

2. A happy, successful family is not an accident—it requires careful planning. Proverbs 24:3, 4, Amplified, says, "Through skillful and godly Wisdom is a house [a life, a home, a family] built, and by understanding it is established [on a sound and good foundation]. And by knowledge shall the chambers [of its every area] be filled with all precious and pleasant riches."
   How can you apply this verse to raising a family? _____
   _____

3. Who should be the foundation of your home? (See 1 Corinthians 3:11 and Matthew 7:24-27.)

4. How does Proverbs 24:3, 4 describe this foundation?
   _____

5. With what is this house filled (Proverbs 24:3, 4)? _____
   _____

Your home can be a loving shelter; a safe place where each member of the family can find comfort, encouragement, and fulfillment, as it is established upon Jesus Christ.

The Greatest Need

6. It has been said that the greatest thing you as a parent can do for your children is to love your spouse. In what areas do you need to:
   a. show outward affection and love for your spouse?
      _____
   b. build up your spouse verbally (through praise, verbal support, and encouragement)? _____
      _____
   c. demonstrate oneness as a couple? _____
      _____
   d. put your spouse's needs and interests first in the family?
      _____

7. How does love for your spouse build security into your child? _____
   _____

Parental Attitudes

8. Psalm 127:3 presents the biblical attitude toward children. Children are a _____ from God. How would this attitude affect the way children are raised? _____
   _____

9. Discuss the following concept: "Our children are the 'loan of a life' from God."
10. An example of this attitude is found in 1 Samuel 1.

Describe:
a. Hannah's desire _____
b. Hannah's commitment _____
_____
c. Hannah's action _____
d. Hannah's blessings (1 Samuel 2:18-21, 26) _____
_____

What application do you see here as parents? _____
_____
_____

11. List several attributes or characteristics which you feel are essential for a good parent to develop.
    a. _____
    b. _____
    c. _____
    d. _____
    e. _____
    Underline those you need in your life.

12. It is not only hard to be a perfect parent, it is impossible! However, as we depend on God's wisdom and his power to change us, we can become godly people and parents.

    God desires the home to reflect his love and forgiveness, his grace and power. It takes time, work, planning, sacrificing of one's own rights and desires, and total dependence on God. But it is worth the cost!

Prayer

O God, thank you for the beautiful privilege of being a parent. My desire is to build my home on Jesus Christ. May I realize my children belong to you and my responsibility is to nurture, mold, and train them according to your Word. Thank you that you promise to be sufficient for my every need as a parent. Amen.

Recommended Book

Edith Schaeffer, *What Is A Family* (Old Tappan, New Jersey: Revell, 1975)

Lesson Two
Parental Responsibilities

Gone are the days when we can leave the responsibility for raising our children to the school, the church, the neighbors, or the television. If we let our children grow up like weeds without careful planning and the proper influences, they will indeed turn out "wild." Rather than be passive and attack a problem after it arises, we need to provide preventive parenting. Let's be on the offensive to prevent problems from developing in the first place!

1. List the basic parental responsibilities you see in these Scripture verses.
   a. Deuteronomy 6:4-9 _____
   _____
   b. 1 Samuel 12:23 _____
   c. Proverbs 22:6 _____
   d. 1 Timothy 5:8 _____
   e. Titus 2:4-8 _____
2. From Luke 2:52, describe the four areas in which Jesus grew and matured. _____
   _____

   This is the well-balanced life! List what you are doing in each of these areas to help your child develop. _____
   _____
   _____
   _____
   _____

17

Follow in My Footprints

3. Children are great imitators! To a large extent you will reproduce your life through your children (your values, life style, priorities, and character). Realizing this, write a brief paragraph of your responsibility as a parent. _____
   _____
   _____

4. What responsibility do we have as examples to our children from these Scripture verses?
   a. Deuteronomy 4:9, 10: _____
   b. Philippians 3:17: _____
   c. 2 Thessalonians 3:6-9: _____
   d. 1 Timothy 4:12: _____
   Give a specific illustration of how you have been a good or bad example to your child recently.

5. What influence did these parents have on their children?

                                      Parent   *Influence*
   a. Genesis 7:7; 9:1: _____
   b. Genesis 20:1-11; 26:1-10: _____
   c. 1 Samuel 1:27, 28; 2:18, 26: _____
   d. 1 Kings 22:51, 52: _____
   e. 2 Chronicles 20:31, 32: _____
   f. 2 Timothy 1:5; 3:15: _____

6. Exodus 20:4-6 tells us that our iniquities can be passed on to future generations. How? They can be passed on through weaknesses in our basic temperament (by inheritance) and also through our daily example and influence. Describe the effect these sins might have on our children spiritually:
   a. being critical of the pastor or church
   b. gossiping about other Christians
   c. indulging in anger or hurt feelings
   d. bitterness and unforgiveness toward others

e. neglecting your family by putting the church or job first in time and priority
   f. pride over spiritual position or gifts
   g. lusts of the flesh (sexual, material, overeating, etc.)
   h. lack of ethics
   Circle any you are presently experiencing.
7. What kind of example are you being to your child in these areas:

                         Good   *Poor*

   a. prayer
   b. Bible reading and study
   c. Bible memory
   d. consistent life, holiness
   e. using spiritual gifts
8. What characteristics are given here of spiritual leaders?
   a. 1 Timothy 3:2-5, 8-13: _____

   b. Titus 1:6-9: _____

   How does the way a leader manages his home (children) tie in with spiritual positions and responsibilities? ____

Parental Priesthood

9. You as parents are the spiritual priests in your household. You present God to your child, and your child to God. List some ways you could function as the spiritual priest to your family. (See Hebrews 7:25; 1 Peter 2:9; Deuteronomy 6:4-9.)

   a. _____
   b. _____
   c. _____
   d. _____

10. List the spiritual responsibilities toward children which are given in these verses:
    a. Deuteronomy 6:4-9: _____
    b. Matthew 19:13, 14; 18:2-4: _____
    c. 2 Timothy 3:15: _____
    d. Ephesians 6:4: _____
11. What is the ultimate purpose of spiritual training? _____
12. To evaluate: What is one specific area I can change this week to become more effective as a parent?

Prayer

Lord, forgive me for the many times I have been a poor example to my children. Help me to fulfill my spiritual responsibilities through my example and teaching. Thank you for the guidance and instruction your Word provides. Amen.

Recommended Book

Larry Christensen, *The Christian Family* (Minneapolis: Bethany Fellowship, 1970)

Lesson Three
Discipling Your Child

A disciple is a follower. Discipling involves teaching both by example and verbal communication. What an opportunity we have in our homes to disciple our children for Jesus Christ. This should be one of our main priorities in life.

The Covenant Relationship

1. God desires the whole family unit to experience salvation. In the Bible a covenant relationship is set forth dealing with the believer's family. Complete the following verses (taken from the *New American Standard Bible*).
   a. (Noah) Genesis 7:1: "Enter the ark, you and all your _____ (See also Hebrews 11:7.)
   b. (Abraham) Genesis 17:7: "And I will establish My covenant between Me and you and your _____ after you. . . ."
   c. (Jacob) Genesis 28:14: ". . . and in you and in your _____ shall all families of the earth be blessed."
   d. (Joshua) Joshua 24:15: ". . . but as for me and my _____, we will serve the Lord."

2. The Passover Lamb was slain by the father for his family. By faith the father applied the blood to the door and his family was saved (Exodus 12). The whole family was blessed and protected and saved through the father's faith.

The Christian parent can by faith claim the cleansing and protecting blood of Jesus Christ for his household.

The Israelite children were also taught by their father that they belonged to a redeeming God.

3. Summarize these New Testament examples of the believing *household*.

   Who is included:

   a. Acts 16:14, 15: _____
   b. Acts 16:31-34: _____
   c. Acts 18:8: _____

4. If you believe God desires your child to be of his covenant, how will this affect the way you raise your child? _____
   _____

5. Of what importance is the parent's faith for his child? How will children be influenced by the active faith of the parent? _____
   _____

6. Matthew 19:14 tells us not to hinder the children from coming to Christ. In what ways might we hinder our children spiritually? _____
   _____

Leading Your Child to Christ

7. As believing parents, we are appointed to lead our child to personally experience salvation. Do everything possible to lead your child to Christ, but be sensitive to each child's needs, and God's timing. Watch for your opportunities to talk about the Lord to your child. Here are some suggested steps in leading your child to Christ. (Use the Bible. Let him read the verses if he can. Explain what each verse means.)

   a. Tell your child how much God loves him (John 3:16).

   b. Explain why your child needs to be saved (Rom. 3:23; 6:23).
   c. Remind your child what Christ has done for him (Romans 5:8; 1 Peter 2:24).
   d. Tell your child that he must personally ask Christ to come into his life as Savior and Lord (John 1:12; Revelation 3:20).
   e. Teach your child that he can daily appropriate God's forgiveness (1 John 1:7, 9).

Sample Prayer

Dear Jesus, thank you for your love, and for dying on the cross for me. Forgive me for my sin. Come into my life to be my Savior and Lord. Thank you that you will never leave me. Amen.

Ask the child what he asked God to do; and how he knows God did it. Each day assure the child of his salvation and relationship to Christ. (Note: For a small child you might want to use the Wordless Book or Child Evangelism glove.)

8. What promises are given in these Scripture verses regarding the eternal status of our salvation?
   a. John 5:24: _____
   b. John 10:28, 29: _____
   c. 2 Timothy 1:12: _____
   d. 1 John 5:11-13: _____

Instruction in the Faith

9. Isaiah 28:10 tells us we are to continuously and repeatedly teach God's Word to our children.
What are some results of teaching God's Word to your children?
   a. Deuteronomy 4:8-13: _____
   b. Psalm 119:9, 11: _____
   c. 1 Timothy 4:12, 16: _____

11. List and discuss possible types of meaningful family worship for the following age groups. Be creative! (See the recommended list of books for additional ideas.)
    a. Toddlers (3 months to 3 years): _____
    _____
    b. Preschool (4, 5 years): _____
    _____
    c. Primary (Grades 1-3): _____
    _____
    d. Junior (Grades 4-6): _____
    _____
    e. Junior High (Grades 7-9): _____
    _____
    f. High School and Adult: _____
    _____

12. To evaluate: How can I improve our family worship?

Prayer

God my Father, by faith I believe you have called my family to experience your salvation. May I claim the protection and cleansing of your blood for each of my children. Help me to lead my children into a saving knowledge of Christ. Help us to worship you as a family and grow together in our faith. Amen.

Recommended Books

Lois Bock and Miji Working, *Happiness Is a Family Time Together* (Old Tappan, N.J.: Fleming Revell Co., 1975)
    also: *Happiness Is A Family Walk with God, 1977*
Andrew Murray, *How to Raise Your Children for Christ* (Minneapolis: Bethany Fellowship, 1975)
Sharee and Jack Rogers, *The Family Together* (Los Angeles: Action House, 1976)
Betsey Scanlan, *Family Bible Study Book* #1, #2 (Old Tappan, N.J.: Fleming Revell Co., 1977)

Ruth Johnson, *Devotions for the Family* #1, #2 (Chicago: Moody Press, 1956)

John C. Souter, James O'Brosky, *A Family Hour Notebook, Getting to Know God* (Irvine, Ca.: Harvest House, 1978)

Called to Develop & Train

Lesson Four
Developing Your Child's Self-Esteem

One of the greatest gifts you can give your child is good self-esteem—a feeling of personal worth. It is something he desperately needs. Without it, he faces a life filled with inferiorities, inadequacy, self-hatred, self-doubt, and misery. This lack of personal worth can eventually result in drug abuse, alcoholism, criminality, mental illness, and broken homes. No one else can build the child's self-esteem like the parent!

The Basis for Self-Esteem

When our child is born, we tend to have high parental standards. We want our child to be the prettiest, smartest, and best!

1. Compare the world's values to God's values.

World's Values	*God's Values*
a. physical beauty	a. 1 Peter 3:3, 4
b. intelligence, abilities	b. Hebrews 11:6
c. wealth, status	c. Matthew 22:37-39

    How does God judge man? 1 Samuel 16:7: _____
    What are you as a parent doing to develop God's values in your child? _____

2. The proof of our personal value is that God said it, so it

must be true! Summarize what these verses teach about your value and worth to God.
a. Genesis 1:26: _____
b. Psalm 139:1-18: _____
c. Isaiah 45:9; 64:8: _____
d. Ephesians 2:10: _____
e. 1 Peter 2:5, 9-11: _____
God made us the way we are. He has a unique plan for each of us.

3. God accepts us in Jesus Christ as we are. He provides us with forgiveness and his righteousness. How can we reject what is of God? Briefly summarize how you would communicate this to a child or teenager who is "putting himself down." _____
_____
_____

4. Paul is an example of a person with good self-esteem. Summarize his attitude toward himself from these verses: Romans 12:3; 1 Corinthians 2:1-5; 15:9, 10: 2 Corinthians 12:9, 10; 2 Timothy 4:6-8. _____
_____
_____

Building Your Child's Self-Esteem

5. Love and acceptance are important building blocks for your child's self-love and acceptance. List ten possible ways to verbalize or show your love and acceptance for your child.
   a.   f.
   b.   g.
   c.   h.
   d.   i.
   e.   j.

6. Circle any of the following examples of rejection or aggression of which you are guilty.
   a. name-calling (stupid, clumsy, lazy, dumb, ugly, messy)
   b. ignoring them (not listening, answering, or responding)
   c. continual criticism (of them, their friends, habits, clothes, activities)
   d. physical abuse (discipline done in anger; bodily harm; or failure to meet physical needs)

   What are the results of these actions?

7. One positive way to build our children's self-esteem is to help them to excel in at least one area. This gives them self-confidence and an ability to gain acceptance among their peers. Put each of your children's names next to an area where they are developing skills and abilities.

   a. music
   b. sports
   c. drama
   d. hobbies
   e. art
   f. homemaking
   g. animals
   h. carpentry
   i. academic
   j. electronics
   k. leadership
   l. _____

8. To discuss together:

   Should you force your child to participate in sports if he doesn't want to?

   How can you encourage practicing music lessons without nagging?

   How do you determine your child's area of achievement?

   How involved should you become in school problems?

9. The area of discipline actually is related to self-esteem. What principle is given in Hebrews 12:8? _____
   _____

   Consistent, loving discipline with enforced guidelines is essential for the building of one's self-esteem.

10. Another method by which you can develop your child's self-worth is by encouraging his independence. A child who is overprotected, smothered, waited upon, and

dependent will not experience positive feelings toward himself.

List several ways to gradually develop a child's independence and freedom.

a. ages 2-5: _____

b. ages 6-12: _____

c. ages 13-18: _____

Hope for the Hopeless

11. What hope does Philippians 1:6 give us? _____

    How can you use this verse to encourage your child?
12. During adolescence a child's self-esteem often hits an all time low. Be aware of their needs at this crucial time.

Prayer

Thank you, Lord, for each of my children—just as they are. Help me to encourage and praise them. May they sense their worth and value to you. As I love and accept them, may they accept themselves. Amen.

Recommended Books

James Dobson, *Hide or Seek* (Old Tappan, N.J.: Revell), 1974
James Dobson, *Preparing for Adolescence* (Santa Ana, Ca.: Vision House), 1978

Lesson Five
Developing Character and Values

"He doesn't pick up his toys."
"I can't trust her. She lies to me."
"She is running around with the wrong gang."
"He is selfish and doesn't think about anyone else."
"He just lies around and won't get a job."

Do any of these sound familiar? Developing character begins at an early age and truly determines a person's effectiveness, spiritual potential, and future happiness.

Character Qualities

1. What are several character traits you would like to see developed in your child? _____
   _____

2. The Book of Proverbs gives us some excellent, practical guidelines in developing character in our children. Name the character trait mentioned in these verses and give one example of how you can help develop it in your child.
   a. Proverbs 1:7, 2:5, 17: _____

   b. Proverbs 3:13, 14; 10:13: _____

   c. Proverbs 10:4, 5; 12:9, 11, 24: _____

   d. Proverbs 16:32; 25:28: _____

   e. Proverbs 10:10 (see TLB): _____

   f. Proverbs 12:13, 17: _____

3. Proverbs 20:11, TLB, says, "The character of even a child can be known by the way he acts—whether what he does is pure and right." What do a child's actions reveal? _____
_____

4. The source of godly character is the Holy Spirit. As we are filled with and controlled by the Holy Spirit, what evidences are seen in our lives? Claim Galatians 5:22, 23 for your children.

Outer Influences

5. Your child will become like his friends. As he grows older he is influenced progressively more by his peers and less by his parents. (See Proverbs 27:19.)

6. How do Proverbs 13:20; 17:17 describe the influence of friends? _____
Name three specific things you can do to influence your child's choice of friends. _____
_____

7. What two areas of temptation is a young man (or girl) warned about?
   a. Proverbs 5:1-6; 6:26; 2:16-19: _____
   b. Proverbs 23:19-21, 29-35: _____
How will these affect his character? _____
_____

8. What can you as a parent do to protect your child from these temptations as he grows toward adulthood?
_____
_____

Sex Education

9. It is important from an early age to give your child a Christian perspective on sex. Read some of the recommended books. How do you rate yourself on sex education?

	Yes	No
a. I have taught my child God's beautiful plan for sex on his level of understanding.	____	____
b. I am honest in answering questions.	____	____
c. I have taught scriptural principles regarding moral purity to my older children.	____	____
d. I have taught my child the proper names of the parts of the body and their functions.	____	____
e. I am sensitive to outside influences my child is experiencing regarding sex.	____	____
f. I have a healthy, fulfilling sex life with my spouse.	____	____

Teaching Responsibility

10. Many young people today lack a sense of responsibility. Discuss the following areas together.
    a. How do you teach a child to work?
    b. Discuss typical household chores and responsibilities.
    c. How do you motivate a child to take responsibility?
    d. What about allowances or monetary reinforcements?
    e. How do you teach tithing?
11. List several possible ways to develop responsibility in the following age groups:
    a. ages 2-5 _____

    b. ages 6-12: _____

    c. ages 13-18: _____

12. What two things do you plan to do this week to help develop your child's character? _____
   _____
   _____

Prayer

Lord, sometimes I am too tired to enforce my standards and rules. Sometimes it is easier to clean up my child's mess than teach him to be responsible. Give me the physical strength and inner stamina to teach my children responsibility and develop their character. Lord, I want them to reflect Christ in their lives. Amen.

Recommended Books

E. Margaret Clarkson, *Susie's Babies* (Grand Rapids, Mich.: Wm. Eerdmans Publications, 1960)

Dr. James Dobson, *Preparing for Adolescence* (Santa Ana, Ca.: Vision House, 1978)

Letha Scanzoni, *Sex Is a Parent Affair* (Glendale, Ca.: Regal Books, 1973)

Charles R. Swindoll, *You and Your Child* (Nashville, Tenn.: Thomas Nelson Inc., Publishers, 1977)

Lesson Six
Developing Your Child's Uniqueness and Gifts

It seems no matter how many children one has, each is a unique individual! No two are exactly alike. It certainly adds variety and interest to the home. This situation can also cause problems as we try to understand a child who is quite different from ourselves.

Adaptable Training

1. Read Proverbs 22:6 in several versions. Charles Swindoll[1] paraphrases it as, "Adapt the training of your child so that it is in keeping with his God-given characteristics and tendencies; when he comes to maturity, he will not depart from the training he has received."
2. What is the command in this verse? _____
   _____
3. What is the promise? _____
4. List several means of knowing your child so you can train him according to his God-given tendencies.
   a.
   b.
   c.
   d.

---

1. Charles Swindoll, *You and Your Child* (Nashville, Tenn.: Thomas Nelson Inc., Publishers, 1977), p. 27. Used by permission.

One of a Kind

5. Beverly LaHaye's book, *How to Develop Your Child's Temperament*[2] discusses the four basic temperaments and how they are manifested in your child. Why is it important to understand your child? _____
_____

6. Write a brief paragraph on each of your children (use additional paper if needed), summarizing their strengths and weaknesses and basic temperament tendencies as you see them today. _____
_____
_____
_____
_____
_____
_____

    Begin praising your child for the strengths and spiritual qualities you discovered.

7. Are you aware of interests and tendencies which are developing toward a particular vocation or life work for your child?
    How can you encourage these interests? _____
_____
_____

8. List specific ways you need to change your handling of a particular child. _____
_____
_____

Your Child Is Gifted!

9. The Bible says God has given each of his children spiritual gifts. Summarize these verses.

35

    a. 1 Corinthians 12:7: _____
    b. Ephesians 4:7: _____
    c. 2 Timothy 1:6: _____
    d. 1 Peter 4:10: _____
10. List all the gifts of the Holy Spirit as given in Romans 12 and 1 Corinthians 12. Ask the Lord to give you discernment and sensitivity in being aware of your child's spiritual gifts. Circle the gifts you already see developing in your older children. _____
_____
_____
_____
_____
_____

11. What is the purpose of spiritual gifts?
    a. 1 Corinthians 12:7: _____
    b. 1 Peter 4:11c: _____
12. Ask the Lord to help you develop your child's spiritual gifts and ministries. Encourage your child in activities which could enhance his gifts. Pray that God will keep your child sensitive to the Holy Spirit and available for his use.

Prayer

Thank you, Lord, for the uniqueness of each of my children. May I be a positive influence in helping them develop their full potential for Jesus Christ. Amen.

Recommended Book

Rick Yohn, *Discover Your Spiritual Gift and Use It* (Wheaton, Ill.: Tyndale House Publishers, 1975)

---

2. Beverly LaHaye, *How to Develop Your Child's Temperament* (Irvine, Ca.: Harvest House)

Called to Discipline
Lesson Seven
Disciplining Toward Obedience

Discipline is training. It implies molding, correcting, instructing, and drilling. It should ultimately result in self-discipline and self-control. This will produce a child who is obedient to God and disciplined in his life style.

Parental Authority

Many parents do not realize their God-given position of authority. They are afraid to discipline! God holds you accountable and responsible for disciplining your children. It is not optional!

1. What command is given to children in Exodus 20:12 and Colossians 3:20? Is this dependent upon the parents' perfection? _____
   _____

2. How does Hebrews 12:9 establish the parent's authority?
   _____

3. Why is it important to teach your child to respect authority figures? _____
   How can you accomplish this? _____
   _____

4. Every child is born with a fallen (sinful) nature. It is normal for a child to challenge his parents' authority even

from the age of sixteen months or sooner. Discuss together:

How could a parent lose confrontations with a small toddler?

What does this do to the child's respect for the parents?

How do small babies and toddlers manipulate their parents?

How do older children manipulate their parents?

Godly Discipline

5. What is evidenced by loving discipline (Proverbs 13:24; Hebrews 12:6)? _____
   Do you love your child enough to follow through with consistent, godly discipline?
6. What purpose in godly discipline is given in these Scripture verses?
   a. Psalm 119:67, 71: _____
   b. Proverbs 19:18: _____
   c. Proverbs 20:30: _____
   d. Proverbs 23:13, 14: _____
   e. Hebrews 12:10: _____
7. What is God's appointed instrument in discipline?
   a. Proverbs 22:15; 29:15: _____
   Discuss the advantages of using this rather than your hand. Also, what is the value of a measure of pain?
8. Dr. James Dobson[1] recommends mild spankings to begin soon after a year. Others believe you should start sooner. What do these verses suggest regarding the importance of early discipline?
   a. Proverbs 13:24: _____
   b. Proverbs 19:18: _____
9. What place do "distractions" have in training the small toddler? _____

---

1. Dr. James Dobson, *The Strong-Willed Child* (Wheaton, Ill., Tyndale House Publishers, Inc., 1978), p. 46.

10. Larry Christensen says we are to spank our child when dealing with disobedience, rebellion, and stubbornness.[2] Give an example of one of these three areas for:
    a. toddlers or preschoolers: _____
    _____
    _____
    b. ages 6-12: _____
    _____
    _____
    c. ages 13-18: _____
    _____
    _____

    If a small child is taught to obey his parents he will not have to be disciplined as frequently when he is older. He will develop an obedient spirit as a young child with his self-will under control.

11. What are some results of good discipline?
    a. Proverbs 23:13, 14: _____
    b. Proverbs 29:17: _____
    c. Ephesians 6:1-4: _____

12. Forgiveness and reconciliation is an important aspect of discipline. Following a spanking, the child should be physically loved and told that he is forgiven. Pray with him. It can be a warm, sensitive time together. A child's heart is especially tender after correctly administered discipline.

Prayer

Lord, sometimes it is difficult to discipline my disobedient child. Help me to realize my God-given responsibilities as a parent to lovingly discipline this precious child you have given

---

[2]. Larry Christensen, *The Christian Family* (Minneapolis: Bethany Fellowship), p. 116

me. May you touch his inner spirit and give him the desire to obey. Amen.

Recommended Books

James Dobson, *Dare to Discipline* (Wheaton, Ill.: Tyndale House Publishers, Inc., 1970)

Lesson Eight
Disciplining Older Children

An obedient child is a happy child! Characteristics of a child who is disciplined in a loving, consistent manner are security and stability, a sense of feeling loved, self-esteem, confidence, and respect for authority.

Biblical Discipline

1. Read Hebrews 12:5-11.
   a. Whom does God discipline? _____
   b. Why? _____
   c. What are the results? _____
   d. How has God disciplined you in recent years? _____
   _____
   _____

2. In Hebrews 5:8 what did Jesus learn regarding discipline?
   _____

3. We have a sad commentary on the fatherhood of Eli the priest in 1 Samuel. Read 1 Samuel 2; 3:12-14.
   a. What was Eli's mistake? _____
   b. What resulted from his mistake? _____
   _____

4. What lesson do you see for yourself as a parent? _____
   _____

The unrestrained, disobedient, and rebellious tyrant of

two years of age will become the defiant, uncontrollable, and rebellious adolescent of tomorrow.

5. How should you handle talking back, sassing, and verbal abuse by a child? (Review Lesson 7.) _____
_____

6. How should direct disobedience or rebelliousness of a child aged 6-12 years be handled? _____
_____

7. Is there any place for nagging, threatening, verbal put-downs, hostility, withdrawing of love, yelling, or physical abuse as discipline? Immediate discipline with the "rod" removes this approach.

8. What warnings are given to parents? Summarize these verses.
   a. Proverbs 11:29: _____
   b. Ephesians 6:4: _____
   c. Colossians 3:21: _____
   How can unfair discipline result in bitterness?
   How can you prevent disciplining in anger?
   Give one example of an attitude or action to avoid.

Other Forms of Discipline

9. As the child grows older, sometimes a form of social restriction or withdrawal of privileges is most effective for certain types of misbehavior. Match possible discipline tactics with behavior problems.

Discipline Tactics	*Behavior Problems*
no playing outside with friends	disobeying rules
no TV	fighting with siblings
no allowance	unfinished homework
sent to room	irresponsibility
other: _____	_____

10. Through positive reinforcement, we can often prevent discipline problems by motivating good behavior. Possi-

ble motivations or rewards include verbal praise, monetary gain, a special treat, stars on a chart, etc. These are especially effective in developing consistent habits in self-care and grooming, care of the child's room and clothes, jobs around the house, feeding animals, practicing an instrument, or developing good study habits.

a. For what ages would this be most effective? _____
_____

b. What do you see as the strengths and weaknesses of these tactics? _____
_____
_____

(See *Dare to Discipline*, chapter 2, for more discussion in this area.)

11. Why is it important that parents be in agreement regarding discipline? _____
_____

12. As we physically discipline our children, we need to pray for their inner life. Spanking controls behavior, but only God can change the spirit. Claim Ezekiel 11:19, "I will give you one heart and a new spirit; I will take from you your hearts of stone and give you tender hearts of love for God" (TLB). Pray for their wills, that God would give them the desire to obey (Philippians 2:13). Pray for a spirit of obedience toward you and toward God. Ask for a cleansing and deliverance of a rebellious spirit. List each child below as you pray for them in a specific area.

_____
_____
_____
_____
_____

Prayer

Lord, surely you are honored and glorified by obedience in my life. Even so, Lord, may each of my children develop an obedient spirit in his life. Help me to be consistent and confident as I discipline my children according to your Word. Amen.

Recommended Books

Larry Christensen, *The Christian Family* (Minneapolis: Bethany Fellowship, 1970)

James Dobson, *Dare to Discipline* (Wheaton, Ill.: Tyndale House Publishers, Inc., 1970)

Lesson Nine
Special Discipline Problems

The goal in disciplining our children should always be kept in view—that of spiritual maturity and self-discipline. With certain ages or particular types of problems, the challenges involved can be overwhelming!

Standards and Rules

All competitive games have certain guidelines and rules. Our homes need guidelines and rules to govern behavior. These provide security and stability as well as preventing misunderstandings or inconsistent discipline.

1. List several rules in your home which you feel are well understood by your children. _____
   _____
   _____
2. List one rule which is difficult to enforce. _____
   _____
   Is this rule unjust or unreasonable?
   Why can't you enforce it?
3. Expect obedience from your children! Have as few rules as possible, but follow through on them. Don't be wishy-washy or a "soft touch." Your child will lose respect for you and try to manipulate you.

Your Walk with the Lord

4. Summarize how these verses apply to parents.
    a. 1 Corinthians 13:4-8: _____
    _____
    b. Isaiah 40:31: _____
    c. Colossians 2:6, 7: _____
    d. Ephesians 4:30-32: _____
    e. Ephesians 3:16-21: _____
    f. 2 Peter 1:5-9: _____
5. Read Colossians 3 from the viewpoint of a parent. In what areas did the Lord speak to you regarding your relationship to your child? _____
_____

6. What is the greatest spiritual need in your life as a parent?
_____

7. Read at least one recommended book that relates to a particular interest or problem you have in child rearing.
    Now, choose the area(s) with which you are most concerned for your particular situation.

The Strong- (Self-) Willed Child

8. Special needs which the strong- (self-) willed child has are: to be taught obedience as a small child; to be reassured of your love; to experience the consequences of his behavior; to have his will shaped; to accept Christ at an early age.
    a. Describe a recent confrontation with your child in which you followed through with authoritative, firm leadership. _____
    _____
    b. How do you reward his obedience? _____
    _____
    c. How are you praying for your child? _____
    _____

d. What areas cause the greatest conflicts? What can be done to eliminate or resolve these conflicts? _____
_____

The Handicapped or Retarded Child

9. Special needs of the handicapped or retarded child in disciplining are: repetition; longer time span for obedience; closer supervision; more parental patience and love; consistent and firm rules; and strong self-acceptance.
   a. What area of discipline is your greatest problem with your handicapped or retarded child? _____
   _____
   b. What personal attitude causes you the greatest problem?
   _____
   c. Have you sought professional help in handling your child or in providing him with the greatest possible opportunities and experiences to develop his potential?

Hyperactive Child

10. Special needs for the hyperactive child include: a calm, relaxed environment; repetition of rules; consistent, firm rules; a structured routine; and following through on commands.
    a. Have you sought professional help in finding a possible cause for the problem? (emotional, brain damage, diet, etc.)
    b. How does discipline provide security for this type of child? _____
    c. Have you dealt with any guilt on your part over "failure" as a parent?
    d. Have you considered the use of medication for your child?
    e. How are you working with his teacher at school?

Teens

11. Special needs which you face in raising teenagers include: developing gradual independence toward freedom; guidelines for behavior; availability to their needs; respect and trust; understanding; and building their self-esteem and self-acceptance.
    a. Does your child know what you expect of him? Discuss your rules and boundaries with him.
    b. Discuss ways of disciplining a teenager, such as withholding privileges, grounding him, etc.
    c. List several areas in which you need to communicate with your child. Begin communicating in one area this week. _____
    _____
    d. Discuss with your child dating standards and guidelines which you feel are important.

Single Parenting

12. The child of a single parent needs: security and love; identity with an adult of the same sex as his absent parent"; reassurance and help in dealing with any guilt he has over the loss of a parent; and quality time geared especially for him.
    a. Have you as a parent dealt with any anger, bitterness, self-pity, resentment, or hatred over the loss of your partner? This is one of the greatest things you can do for your child.
    b. What is your weakest point as a single parent? How can you change in this area? _____
    _____
    _____
    c. What involvement do you have with other families, friends, and adults who can help minister to your child's needs? _____
    _____

Prayer

God, may I keep a positive perspective as a parent. When problems arise with my children, may I see these as a challenge to grow in my relationship to you. Help me to have a sensitive and teachable spirit. Thank you that your grace is sufficient for my needs. Amen.

Recommended Books

Dr. James Dobson, *Dare to Discipline* (Wheaton, Ill.: Tyndale House Publishers, Inc., 1970)

Dr. James Dobson, *The Strong-Willed Child* (Wheaton: Tyndale, 1978)

Evelyn Millis Duvall, *Parent and Teenager Living and Loving* (Nashville, Tenn.: Broadman Press, 1976)

Bill McKee, *Shut Your Generation Gap* (Wheaton: Tyndale, 1970)

Ben F. Feingold, M.D., *Why Your Child Is Hyperactive* (New York, NY.: Random House, 1974)

Charles R. Swindoll, *You and Your Child* (Nashville: Thomas Nelson Inc., Publishers, 1977)

Called to Completion
Lesson Ten
Family Oneness

The Christian home can be a place where its members experience the security and freedom to develop their own unique individuality. It should also be a safe place where acceptance and forgiveness are lovingly offered. The family has the opportunity to provide healing from life's hurts and traumas to each other. Trust, oneness, and wholeness will result.

1. What do you feel are characteristics of an ideal family?
   _____
   _____

It's Tradition!

2. Family traditions and customs can help bind a family together through joyfully shared experiences and activities. Traditions help develop security and stability within the family unit. Check traditions or activities listed below which you now enjoy. Circle three additional ones you would like to try.

family birthday celebrations	family devotions
family picture night	picnics, excursions
prayer time together	Christmas traditions
musical evening	other holiday customs
reading a book together aloud	entertaining as a family

gardening together   athletic involvement as a
                          family
game night   raising pets
crafts done together   hobbies
dinner time sharing   family contests

Dissension Breeds Disunity

3. a. What attitudes caused dissension in the family of Isaac (Genesis 27)? _____
   b. What resulted (Genesis 27:41-46)? _____
   c. What caused a lack of oneness in Joseph's family (Genesis 37)? _____
   d. What resulted? _____

Working Things Out

4. a. In Luke 15:11-32, what was involved in restoring the relationship between father and son? _____
   b. What action did Hannah take to help her overcome her feelings of bitterness and despondency in 1 Samuel 1:1-20? _____
5. The proper understanding of roles within a family helps to develop oneness and peacefulness. To whom is each family member responsible?
   husband (Ephesians 5:25, 1 Corinthians 11:3): _____
   wife (Ephesians 5:22-24): _____
   children (Ephesians 6:1-3): _____
6. The key to happy family relationships is found in Ephesians 5:21. How could this be enacted? _____

7. Who is our example (1 Corinthians 11:3, Philippians 2:5)? _____ The dominant characteristic of a godly home should be loving servanthood to each other.

One in the Spirit

8. Ephesians 4:3 says, "being diligent to preserve the unity of the Spirit in the bond of peace" (NASB).
   What does diligence imply? _____
   If family unity is on a spiritual level, how can it be maintained (or obtained)? _____
   _____

9. What blessings result from family unity (Psalm 133:1-3)?
   _____

10. What command is given in Ephesians 5:18? _____
    _____
    How would this affect the quality of family relationships?
    _____

11. It is the responsibility of the parents to be filled and controlled by the Holy Spirit. List characteristics of the Spirit-filled home (Galatians 5:22-26). _____
    _____
    _____
    Compare characteristics of the home which is controlled by sin (Galatians 5:19-21). _____
    _____

12. We have looked at various factors involved in developing family unity—family traditions, working through dissension, understanding roles, mutual submission and servanthood, working at unity, and being controlled by the Holy Spirit. Ultimately the family's oneness and wholeness depends upon the parents' spiritual relationship to God and how that relationship is translated to others in the home.

Prayer

Dear Lord, I truly desire oneness and unity in my home. May I be sensitive to the needs of other family members. May your spirit of peace prevail in our midst as we seek to center our home on Jesus Christ. Amen.

Recommended Books

Tim & Bev LaHaye, *Spirit-Controlled Family Living* (Old Tappan, N.J.: Revell Co., 1978)

Edith Schaeffer, *What Is a Family?* (Old Tappan, N.J.: Revell, 1975)

H. Norman Wright & Rex Johnson, *Characteristics of a Caring Home* (Santa Ana, Ca.: Vision House Publishers, 1978)

Lesson Eleven
Preparation for Independence

Many families experience trauma when the children begin to leave the nest. Either the children are not prepared for the responsibilities and obligations of independence or the parents are not prepared to properly release their child to a life of his own. The act of relinquishing your children actually begins the day they are born.

Preparing to Fly

1. Study these parental examples of releasing children. What did you learn from each one?
   a. Genesis 22: _____
   b. 1 Samuel 1: _____
   c. Luke 2:41-52: _____
   d. Luke 15:11-32: _____
2. What is the basis for our philosophy of life (Proverbs 1:1-8; 2:1-6)? _____

3. How can you help your child develop his own values and spiritual principles (Deuteronomy 6:4-9; 1 Timothy 4:12)? _____

After pouring twenty years of teaching and training into his life, can you relinquish him to God and fully trust God to complete his work in your child?

4. How does teaching children to accept responsibilities relate to a productive adult life? _____
_____

5. Check the following areas in which children 6-12 years old should be making their own decisions. Circle additional areas where teenagers should be making their own decisions. Put an "X" where you feel they might still need parental guidance.
   a. choosing what clothes to wear
   b. choosing their own friends
   c. choosing how to manage their own money
   d. choosing what activities to become involved in
   e. choosing their own TV programs
   f. buying their own clothes
   g. choosing church attendance or involvement
   h. choosing a life vocation or college major
   i. choosing a life partner

6. Here are some Christian principles involved in making decisions.
   a. Does it glorify God (Corinthians 6:19, 20)?
   b. Is it a good witness (Acts 1:8)?
   c. Is it helpful to me—can I do it in the name of Christ (Colossians 3:17)?
   d. How do my parents feel about this (Exodus 20:12; Colossians 3:20)?

Leaving the Nest

7. In what ways are you preparing your child to choose his life vocation? Circle areas in which you could improve:
   a. developing his natural talents and abilities
   b. exposing him to a variety of jobs and experiences
   c. guiding him in choosing his school subjects
   d. encouraging him to consider extra education or training

e. teaching him the value and responsibility of work
   f. praying with and for him
   g. discussing together his strengths and weaknesses
8. Are you preparing your child for a happy marriage? Circle areas you need to work on.
   a. providing a good example in your own marriage
   b. giving him adequate and wholesome sex education and guidance
   c. providing practical training such as areas of homemaking for girls and areas of home maintenance and repair for guys
   d. praying for him during his dating years and for his future mate
   e. giving him guidelines in choosing a mate
   f. being available for godly counsel and advice
9. Doors of communication need to be kept wide open during these last years in the nest. Summarize these verses:
   a. Proverbs 17:9: _____
   b. Proverbs 18:13: _____
   c. Ephesians 4:31, 32: _____
   d. James 1:19: _____
10. Name the greatest hindrance to good communication with your child. _____

Solo!

11. Describe the potential danger caused by not cutting emotional ties by the time your child leaves home or marries. Have you experienced any problems in your own marriage or parental relationship because of continuing emotional dependency on your parents?

    Consider possible motivations which cause a parent to hang onto his child after maturity.
12. Perhaps the greatest help in "letting go" of your child is to remember that your child is merely on loan to you for a

period of time to mold, train, and influence. A child is not to *possess* but to *prepare* for a life of his own. The process of breaking away from the parents is normal, natural, and necessary.

Prayer

Dear God, thank you for each precious year with my child. May I be preparing him for maturity and responsibility in his eventual independence. Grant me your grace when that day comes, to fully let him go. Thank you that he is in your loving hands. Amen.

Recommended Book

H. Norman Wright & Rex Johnson, *Characteristics of a Caring Home* (Santa Ana, Ca.: Vision House Publishers, 1978)

Lesson Twelve
Parental Prayers

"Your mother is praying for you" is a wall sign used at some rescue missions to remind "down and outers" of their mother's influence and faithfulness in prayer. Parental prayers have kept many children out of sin and delivered others from its hold. The power of parental prayers must not be minimized.

1. How does Paul pray for his spiritual children in Colossians 1:9-12 and Philippians 1:3-11? _____
   _____
   _____

2. What attitude did Paul experience toward his "children" in 1 Thessalonians 2:7-10? _____
   _____

Promises

3. Tell how the following scriptural promises could be used in your prayers:
   a. Isaiah 49:25d: _____
   b. Isaiah 54:13: _____
   c. Psalm 144:12: _____
   d. Proverbs 20:11: _____
   e. Proverbs 22:6: _____
4. Write a brief prayer for your child using one of the above Scripture verses. _____
   _____
   _____

5. Additional verses to claim for your children:
   a. physical protection (Psalm 34:7; 91:11; 121)
   b. guidance (Psalm 32:8; Proverbs 3:5, 6)
   c. morality, purity (1 Thessalonians 4:7; 1 Corinthians 6:19, 20)
   d. spiritual growth and hunger (Ephesians 3:16, 20; Psalm 42:1, 2)
   e. submissive will (Philippians 2:13; Ephesians 5:20)
   f. Spirit filled (Ephesians 5:18; Luke 11:11-13; John 7:37, 38)
   g. repentance (Psalm 32:1-7; 51)
   h. resistance to sin and temptation (James 4:7; Ephesians 6:10-18; 1 Corinthians 10:13; James 1:12)
   i. strength (Philippians 4:13; Isaiah 40:31)
   j. attitudes (Psalm 51:10)
   k. salvation (1 Timothy 2:4; John 3:16; Romans 1:16)
   l. control of mind (2 Corinthians 10:5)
   m. love (John 13:35; Galatians 5:22; Romans 5:5)
   n. guilt (Romans 8:1, 2; Hebrews 9:14)
   o. forgiveness (Psalm 103:12; Isaiah 44:22; Jeremiah 31:34)
   p. fear (2 Timothy 1:7)
   q. faith (Matthew 17:20; Mark 9:23; Romans 10:17)
   r. deliverance (Luke 4:18)
6. Circle the areas where your children have needs today. Begin claiming these verses for them by faith, believing that God hears and answers prayer.

Try Praise!

7. Verbally praise your child for a positive trait in his character. Be positive.
8. Try praising God for a problem in your child's life and for the troubled child himself. Praise God that he loves your child and desires to do a beautiful thing in his life. Praise

God that he is in control. Then totally relinquish your child into God's loving hands.

On Your Knees

9. In what areas do you personally need prayer in order to become a more godly parent?

priorities	restoring past failures and mistakes
cleansing of sin	victory of temptation
time with God	change in attitudes
character qualities	dependence on God
quality time with children	being controlled by Holy Spirit
relationship with spouse	wisdom in child rearing

10. A prayer time between husband and wife can be a beautiful experience. Suggestions for a productive and refreshing prayer time include:

    honesty

    conversational prayers (short sentence prayers back and forth on one topic at a time)

    confession of sin against each other; asking forgiveness

    prayers of praise and thankfulness for your spouse

11. Susanna Wesley is a good example of a praying mother. She prayed one hour a week for each child, even after they had left home. She bore nineteen children (losing several in infancy), so that was no small task. Some of the results: John was a theologian who was used as a tremendous spiritual force in England; Charles was the greatest hymn writer of all time; and Samuel was a great influence as a poet, teacher, and clergyman.

12. Are you taking advantage of the tremendous power of prayer to influence, mold, and shape your child's life?

Prayer

God, teach me how to pray for my children. Teach me the value of prayer in their lives. Help me to appropriate by faith the beautiful promises you have already given me. Thank you, Lord, for the influence for good I can have in my children's lives through prayer. Amen.

Recommended Books

Evelyn Christensen, *What Happens When Women Pray* (Wheaton, Ill.: Victor, 1975)
Allegra Harrah, *Prayer Weapons* (Old Tappan, N.J.: Fleming Revell, 1975)